THE ARROW FINDS ITS MARK

A Book of Found Poems

Edited by
GEORGIA HEARD

Illustrated by
ANTOINE GUILLOPPÉ

ROARING BROOK PRESS
New York

TABLE OF CONTENTS

INTRODUCTION

Like a sculptor who chisels a block of stone and creates a horse, a head, or a figure, the poets in this anthology have taken words from everyday text and language and refashioned them into poems. These poets scanned the world and found poems in a variety of sources: a photo caption; a note left in a laundry room; Facebook pages and Twitter accounts; an airline magazine; crossword puzzle clues; book titles on a shelf; a dictionary; signs in a hardware store.

To find a poem within the copious amount of text that we encounter every day is the ultimate test of a poet's skill, and not an easy task. If you put a frame around any text and insert line breaks and stanzas—it won't necessarily be a poem. There is something truly magical about transforming words that were originally prose, or, even more of a metamorphosis, utilitarian words (such as in an advertisement), into a poem where language is elevated and deepened by the poet. I believe that creating a found poem has to do with sharpening a poet's vision—seeing that poetry exists all around us and ultimately having the insight and imagination to find it.

The guidelines for creating found poems in *The Arrow Finds Its Mark: A Book of Found Poems* were as follows:

- Poets were asked to find text that already exists in a form other than poetry and present that text as a poem.
- Poets could find poems from any source (other than poetry) including speech or dogs barking as in Sara Holbrook's poem "Weekday Morning Haiku," or bird calls as in J. Patrick Lewis's "A Bird Poetry Reading".
- Poets were encouraged not to change, add, or rearrange words but, as in any creative endeavor, they stretched these guidelines and were allowed to make minor changes in order for the poem to flow more smoothly or make better sense. They could also change punctuation, tense, plurals, and capitalization.
- Poets created their own titles that often gave the poems depth and added another layer of meaning.

- Poets could combine the found poem with another form such as haiku, as in Terry Webb Harshman's "Lake Haiku," or acrostic, as in "Empty Promises" by Kristy Dempsey.

You might be interested in seeing how each poet's process was different: some poets chose to splice words together from a single source and make a kind of word collage, as in Robyn Hood Black's "We See with These"; others took words intact and in order and simply changed the line breaks and added a title, like Avis Harley's "Lawn Talk"; and other poets took words from multiple sources on one theme, as in Bob Raczka's "Places I'd Love to Van Gogh Someday."

During this time of the democratization of words through e-mails, blogs, Twitter, Facebook, and other networking sites, I want my readers to know that poetry is everywhere—if we only look at the world with poet's eyes.

I encourage you to look for poetry where you might not ordinarily think to find it. You'll be surprised at the varied places you just might spot a poem.

FIND A POEM

Find v.
come across
chance upon
stumble on
discover
turn up
bring to light
unearth
locate
encounter
recover
retrieve
regain
get
realize
acquire
find:
find the cheese too strong
find out the truth
the arrow **finds** its mark

Found by George Ella Lyon
in a memo from her son's teacher

MARILYNN'S MONTESSORI MEMO

In connection with the study
of the human body
I borrowed a plastic model
with removable parts.
Unfortunately
I left it out to view
and the heart is missing.

It's about the size
of a dried date
shaped and painted
to look like a heart.
Dear Parents,
If you find it at home
<u>PLEASE</u> <u>PLEASE</u>
return it.

SCHOOL POEMS

FOR LUNCH TODAY

(Facebook status update: Kate—May 6th)
For lunch today:
I had a humiliation sandwich
On critical bread.

For dessert:
I had humble pie ala mode.

WHY I FLUNKED MY TEST

(Facebook status update: Joy—June 10th)
The squirrel was at the window looking in.

AFTER TEST

(Facebook status update: Heather—May 5th)
I think I sprained my spirit.

Found by Patricia Hubbell
in *The New Comprehensive
American Rhyming Dictionary*

A POEM TO SNEAK ONTO THE WALL OF A SCHOOL LUNCHROOM

Fly high,
French fry!

Found by Heidi Bee Roemer
on Twitter, 9/10 by *#itspinkfriday*

IT'S PINK FRIDAY

i'm not wearing pink.

   i guess i

can't sit with you.

4

Found by Rebecca Kai Dotlich
on the website teens.lovetoknow.com

TEXTO

RU0K?
Y/N
BTW
TTLY
BFF
PWB
2DAY
G2G
BCNU
RU0K?

(Translation: ARE YOU OK?/YES/NO/BY THE
WAY/TOTALLY/BEST FRIENDS FOREVER/PLEASE
WRITE BACK/TODAY/GOT TO GO/BE SEEING YOU/
ARE YOU OK?)

Found by Janet Wong
on a box of OxiClean detergent

PEP TALK

Keep cool.

See a brighter solution.

Maintain freshness.

Boost your power!

Found by Lee Bennett Hopkins from selected words in a SPRINT newspaper advertisement

FIRST WINS

FIRST leads.

FIRST moves us forward.

FIRST kicks open the door.

FIRST takes us places
    we've never been
    before.

Nothing comes before FIRST.

FIRST does things
    no one and nothing—
    has ever done.

FIRST isn't later,
    it's now.

What will you do
    FIRST?

Found by Michael Salinger
on signs around the Mentor Hardware Store

THE HARDWARE STORE

Hammer hammer hammer hammer
Hammer hammer
Drill
All purpose
Heavy duty
Wood filler, roto tiller, screws
Saw blades, wing nuts, steel toed shoes
Half off
Items on this shelf
Do it
Do it
Do it
Do it
Do it yourself.

Found by Robyn Hood Black
in Funopolis LASERTAG Results Report,
folded up on a counter in the laundry room

BATTLING BEAMS

CODE NAME: DeathEater

Green Red Blue

you hit 4   7 hit you

you hit 14   5 hit you

you hit 29   8 hit you

BubbaGump, Darth Vader, Terminator,
Megatron, Voldemort, Snape,
Bella Edward Jacob,
Jedi Knight

Green Red Blue

650 shots
Score

X-TREME FUN

Found by Bruce Ballard
on the *New York Times* website asking readers
to post questions to a train operator of
a New York City no. 4 subway line

ASK A TRAIN OPERATO

As a boy I've always
dreamed of being
a subway motorman.
Questions I've always had:

What's the fastest speed you drove your train? How
Why do the trains always start with a jerk? Why do
doors? Can you confirm the existence of *mole*
trains smell like ear wax? Are there days when
it's light outside when you ride in the dark
between the train and the platform? What do you
need to go in reverse? Is it lonely? What gets you

Does it feel	in the tun-
claustro-	nels in the
phobic	dark?

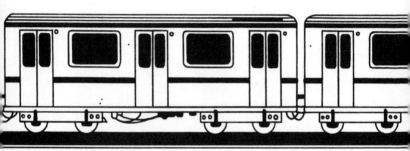

10

often are you tempted to pop a wheelie?
people use the "soccer foot" to catch closing
people living in the tunnels? Why do new
driving a train isn't fun? Do you forget that
all day? Has anyone ever fallen in the gap
do when Mother Nature calls? Do you ever
"excited as a kid" about your job?

What do you
think about
all day?

Is there any way
my dream could
come true?

Found by J. Patrick Lewis
in *All-Time Player Directory,*
Official NBA Encyclopedia

NICKNAMES IN THE NBA

The Mailman, The Admiral, The Answer,
The Truth, The Pearl, The Glove, The Dream,
The Sheriff, The Goods, The Waiter.
Big Ticket, Big Country, Big Smooth,
Big Nasty, Big Baby, Big Fundamental,
Z, Zo, Rip, Bo, Tip, Mo, Pip, Lo, Stro,
Cat, Doggie, Piggie, Goat, Snake, Bull, Horse.
Sam I Am, Tim Bug, Tin Man, Thunder Dan,
Sir Dunks-A-Lot, Boom Dizzle, The Hobbit,
Vinsanity, Mt. Motumbo, White Chocolate,
Vanilla Gorilla, Dollar Bill, Tractor, Scooter,
Ukraine Train, The Owl Without a Vowel,
The Human Highlight Film, Durantula,
Magic, Shaq, Larry Legend, The Chosen One,
His Airness.

Found by Rebecca Kai Dotlich
on *The BIG Box of Magic: A Set of Magic Tricks*

TRICKERY

Magic book.
Magic wand.
Pack of cards.
Escape ball.
Astound friends!
Card tricks.
Coin capers.
Mind reading.
All ages.

Found by Kristy Dempsey
on the Publishers Clearing House
Sweepstakes website homepage

EMPTY PROMISES
(An Acrostic Poem)

Are yo**U** the winner?
We'll be looking . . .
Enter **N**ow,
Become
    a MIL**L**IONAIRE!
Don't wa**I**t!
You never **K**now
    Which **E**ntry could
    Become
The Big Winner.
        Lottery:
Win Instantl**Y**!

ound by Bob Raczka
om computer drop-down menus

HOW TO WRITE A POEM
ON YOUR COMPUTER

nd Table	Repeat Typing	Restart	Restart
ork	Undo Typing	Go To Dictionary	Work
lect All	Repeat Typing	Select Word	Sleep
lete	Undo Typing	Go To Thesaurus	Open Window
	Break	Replace Word	Work
		Delete Word	Sleep
		Break	Close Window
			Quit
			Sleep

Found by Jane Yolen
in Crossword Puzzle Clues,
Daily Hampshire Gazette

CROSS WORDS

NO! NO!
GIVE ME A REASON,
DO SOMETHING!
DON'T ASK ME!
THIS IS FOR REAL . . . !
NO, NO, NO REASON!
SHAME!
DUMP!
DOWN!
SNAKE!

Found by David Harrison
in an *American Airlines* magazine Mensa Quiz

TODAY'S THOUGHT PROBLEM

Jane is
NOW half
her brother Jim's
age.
Three years
ago
she was one –
third his age. Three
yearsfromnow she
will be three-
fifths his
age. HOW
OLD
are they

NOW?

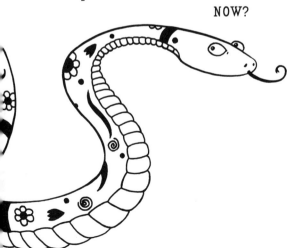

Found by Susan Marie Swanson
in the first entry for the word "light"
in the *American Heritage Dictionary*

THINKING ABOUT *LIGHT* WITH THE DICTIONARY OPEN

Light
may be
the human eye.
The brightness of a lamp.
Illumination.
Daybreak.
A source of fire or awareness.

Understanding.
A way of looking
set on fire.

Found by Naomi Shihab Nye in the
San Antonio Express-News

BREAKING, FROM NORWAY

A radio journalist   quit   on the air
        after complaining   about her job   saying
she   wouldn't read the day's news   because
    "nothing important has happened"
    in the live broadcast   said she was
    "quitting and walking away"
        because she wanted
"to be able to eat properly again
        and   to breathe."

*(Said this to listeners who were presumably breathing
as they listened. Some may even have been eating.)*

She ended   her announcement
        by saying
there wouldn't be any   news
                                Saturday.

Found by Lara Anderson
from book titles on her daughter's
bedroom bookshelf

BOOK HAUNTING

Giants
Ghosts
and Goblins
wait till the moon is
over the house in the night.
Frankenstein
makes a sandwich;
monster soup for the ghost
(a splendid friend, indeed)
that had to go . . .

where the wild things are.

Found by Amy Ludwig VanDerwater
in *Drawing On Both Sides of the Brain*
by Betty Edwards

ARTIST'S ADVICE

Draw everything and anything.
Nothing is unbeautiful:
a few square inches of weeds
a broken glass
a landscape
a human being.
Observe your style.
Guard it.
Put pencil to paper every day.

Found by Bob Raczka
from titles of Van Gogh paintings

PLACES I'D LOVE TO VAN GOGH SOMEDAY

The Yellow House
The Red Vineyard

Beach with Figures and Sea with a Ship
Village Street and Stairs with Figures

Lane with Poplar Trees
Road with Cypress and Star

Field with Poppies
Orchard with Blossoming Plum Trees

Park with a Couple and a Blue Fir Tree
Wheat Field with Crows

The Dance Hall at Arles
Café Terrace at Night

Found by Robyn Hood Black
in crossword puzzle clues in fourth-grade
Sitton Spelling and Word Skills Practice Book

WE SEE WITH THESE

On a clear night, you can see lots of these
sparkling in the sky.

They help you see

Tooth Fairy collectibles,

more than one mouse,

more than one moose,

more than one elf,

more.

23

Found by Paul Janeczko
in *Walden Pond* by Thoreau

WALDEN POND

Walden is a perfect forest mirror:
so fair
so pure
so large
set round with stones
sky water
needs no fence.
A mirror
no stone can crack.
Quicksilver
will never wear off.
No storms.
No dust.
Ever fresh.
A mirror.

Found by Terry Webb Harshman
in a photo caption of this scene near
Branson Davis Road in Randolph County, N.C.
on Wednesday, Sept. 22, 2010

LAKE HAIKU

Hawk perched on a tree
at the Randleman Lake edge . . .
framed by harvest moon.

Found by Joyce Sidman
in the 2010 Greenpeace calendar

SONG OF THE EARTH

Japanese tree frogs
delight in balloon vines.
Standing head to toe, they
absorb water without drinking.

Puffins reuse and recycle
1,000-year-old rocks.
One egg at a time,
they learn to take flight.

Generations of
mother and grandmother orcas
harness the epic power
of their dazzling bodies.

Orangutans sprawl
in ancient forests.
They take turns hugging
the world's most beautiful tree.

The wind returns to the land
with its low, haunting song.
The purpose of the song is not yet clear.

But we are listening.

Found by Joseph Bruchac
in an interview with Hastings Shade,
the Deputy Chief of the Cherokee Nation

JUST LISTEN TO THE ELDERS

There's no secret
to it,
just listen
to the elders.

When they
look at you
they see you—

not just *who*
you are
but *what*
you are

just by
looking
at you.

There's no secret
to it,
just listen
to the elders.

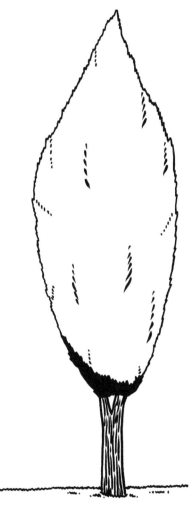

Found by J. Patrick Lewis
in *Placenames of the World* by Adrian Room

LAND OF NOTHING

Land of honest men—Burkina Faso
People of the ten arrows—Hungary
Land of a thousand hills—Rwanda
Land of a million elephants—Laos
Island of the moon—Comoros
Land of forty tribes—Kyrgyzstan
Land of the pure—Pakistan
Land of castles—Catalonia
Abundance of butterflies—Panama
Land of the hummingbird—Trinidad
Land of the eagle—Albania
Land of the lions—Sri Lanka
Land of silver—Argentina
There was gold—Aruba
Land of the thunder dragon—Bhutan
Land of flaming water—Malawi
Big House of Stone—Zimbabwe
Land of the Angles—England
Land of free men—France
Land of the rising sun—Japan
Land of Self-Masters—Uzbekistan
End of the earth—Madagascar
Land of nothing—Namibia

Found by Avis Harley
on a sign in a Shanghai Park
quoted in the *Vancouver Sun*

LAWN TALK:

(Keep off the Grass!)

I love
your
smiles,

but
not
your
foot
on my face!

Found by J. Patrick Lewis
in *The Songs of Wild Birds* by Lang Elliott

A BIRD POETRY READIN

seee-yee-see-yeer, spring-o-the-year
what-cheer, what-cheer, whoit-whoit-
   whoit-whoit
cheer . . . cheerily . . . churee . . . cheer-
   cheerful-charmer
see-wee . . . see-it . . . seedle-ee . . . see-o-
   wit . . . see-yer
oong-k'-choonk, oong-k'-choonk, oong-
   k'-choonk
kick, kick, kidick, kidick, kidick
garuu-tucka-ruuu-tucka-ruuu-tucka
witcha-witcha-witcha-witcha

tull-ull, twirl-erl, whee-oodle
wee-yah, wee-yah, wee-yah weeka-weeka-
    weeka
crack-kokoko
tut-tut, eee-o-lay-leeeeee
tip, tup, zeeeee
conk-la-reee
pee-a-wee . . . ahh-d-dee . . . pee-oh . . .
    pee-a-wee . . . ahh-d-dee . . . pee-oh
tea-cher, tea-cher, TEA-CHER, TEA-CHER
bublo-com seeeee
tea-kettle, tea-kettle, tea-kettle
hoo-awlll

Bird poets, in order of appearance: meadowlark, northern
cardinal, eastern bluebird, red-eyed vireo, American bittern,
Virginia rail, sandhill crane, common snipe, blue jay,
yellow-bellied sapsucker, common raven, wood thrush,
grasshopper sparrow, red-winged blackbird, eastern
wood-pewee, ovenbird, brown-headed cowbird, Carolina
wren, barred owl.

Found by Juanita Havill
in the 2010 Burpee Gardening catalogue

HUMMINGBIRD

Astonishment of tiny

delicate strokes
facing skyward

grace with elegance,
a rare beauty.

Found by Beverly McLoughland
in *The American Robin, A Backyard Institution*,
by Len Eiserer

IN THE NEST

The tiny head
held highest
and the gaping mouth
spread widest
wins the worm.

Found by Beverly McLoughland
in *From the Land, Encounters with*
Natural History, edited by Stephen Trumble

GEESE AT NIGHT

Listen:
Uh-whongk,
Uh-whongk,
Uh-whongk,

And then
you are wide awake
and you smile up
at the ceiling
as the calls fade off
to the north . . .

And already
they are
gone.

Found by Sara Holbrook
every morning at 10:00 am when her dogs, Suzi
and Lili, come face to face with the postman

WEEKDAY MORNING HAIKU

Yarp. Arp. Arp. Arp. Arp.
UNITED STATES POST OFFICE
Arp. Arp. Yarp. Arp. Arp.

Found by David Harrison
in the United Airlines Magazine,
***United Hemispheres*, on a trip from**
Florida back home

HOT-DOGGING

65 canines
entered into
the fifth annual
Lowes Bay Resort
Surf Dog Competition.
A crowd of 2,000
cheers them on.

Dogs
in sunglasses,
Aloha shirts,

ife vests,
swimsuits,
big dogs,
small dogs,
dogs not meant
to swim.
Starting whistle!
Dogs and owners
take to the water
with surfboards
in a chaos of shouts and barks—
"Oscar!" *"Lacey,* come!"
"Chelsea!"

Do they have
all four paws
on the board?
Do they sit
or wag their tails?
Confidence is key.

Many dogs sit casually,
some walk the board
and "ride the nose."
Many simply fall off.

The winner is . . .
Abbie Girl
who wins a free night
at Lowes.

Found by Kristine O'Connell George
in a speech by George Vest—U.S. Senator
from 1879-1903—and one of the leading
orators of his time

MAN'S BEST FRIEND

The one
      absolutely unselfish friend
      that man can have
      is his dog.
A man's dog stands by him,
      will sleep on the cold ground
      if only he may be near
      his master's side.
He is as constant
      in his love
      as the sun in its journey
      through the heavens.
When all other friends desert,
      he remains.

Found by Laura Purdie Salas on a Road Sign in Cumbria, Northern England

THEY DON'T WANT SPEEDING TICKETS, SO . . .

red squirrels
drive slowly

CAUTION
DRIVE
SLOW

Found by Marilyn Singer
in the Pearl River Chinese
zodiac calendar for the Year of the Tiger

YEAR OF THE TIGER

Bright
Ambitious
Short-tempered
Beware of the dog
Talented
Excitable
Vain
Trouble with rabbits
Inventive
Elegant
Impatient
You seek peace
Watch out for dragons

Found by Laura Purdie Salas in book titles on a library shelf

TOP TEN RULES FOR OUR ZOO FIELD TRIP

Don't let the pigeon drive the bus
Please don't feed the bears
Don't go pet a porcupine
Never tease a weasel
Never, ever shout in a zoo
Never smile at a monkey
Please don't wake the animals
Never play snap with a shark
Don't take your elephant to school

DON'T TOUCH THAT!

Found by Rebecca Kai Dotlich
on listology.com

THE END AND GOODBYE

Buhbye
Ta ta
Ciao
Sayanora
Cheerio
Farewell
Later, Gater
Peace out
Adios
Arrivaderci
Hasta la vista
Shoo
Tootles
C U L8R

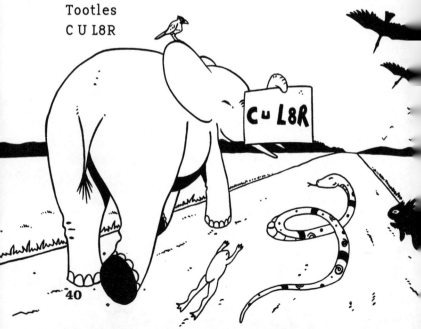

To Leo

Compilation copyright © 2012 by Georgia Heard
Illustrations copyright © 2012 by Antoine Guilloppé
Published by Roaring Brook Press
Roaring Brook Press is a division of
Holtzbrinck Publishing Holdings Limited Partnership
175 Fifth Avenue, New York, New York 10010
mackids.com

Library of Congress Cataloging-in-Publication Data

The arrow finds its mark : a book of found poems / edited by
Georgia Heard ; illustrated by Antoine Guilloppé—1st ed.
   p. cm.
ISBN 978-1-59643-665-7
1. Children's poetry, American.   I. Heard, Georgia.
II. Guilloppé, Antoine, ill.

PS586.3.A77 2012
811'.60809282—dc23

                                              2011017180

Roaring Brook Press books are available for
special promotions and premiums.
For details contact: Director of Special Markets,
Holtzbrinck Publishers.

First edition 2012
Printed in the United States of America
by Worzalla, Stevens Point, Wisconsin

1 3 5 7 9 10 8 6 4 2